THE BUMPER BOOK OF KERRYMAN RIDDLES

**More Books
by
Des MacHale**

THE BUMPER BOOK OF KERRYMAN JOKES
THE BOOK OF CORKMAN JOKES
THE BOOK OF IRISH BULL
THE BOOK OF IRISH LOVE AND MARRIAGE JOKES
THE BOOK OF KERRYMAN JOKES
THE OFFICIAL KERRYMAN JOKE BOOK
THE WORST KERRYMAN JOKES
MORE KERRYMAN JOKES

THE BUMPER BOOK
OF
KERRYMAN RIDDLES

Des MacHale

MERCIER PRESS

Mercier Press
PO Box 5, 5 French Church Street, Cork
24 Lower Abbey Street, Dublin 1

© Des MacHale 1993

ISBN 1 85635 073 8

A CIP is available from the British Library for this book.

For Deirdre, John, Maria and Michael

Printed in Ireland by Litho Press Ltd

INTRODUCTION

For the last twenty-five years or so the most popular joke form (some would say art form) in Ireland has been the Kerryman joke. These jokes were fathered by the Irish Bull out of the Sacred Cow that Kerrymen and Kerrywomen have the best sense of humour in Ireland and are not afraid to laugh at themselves as well as laughing at others.

Undoubtedly, the most popular form of Kerryman joke is the Kerryman riddle, and hence this book. The Kerryman riddle is a two-liner, short, sweet, witty and to the point. It is the joke form of the late twentieth century and will be that of the twenty-first century when people won't have the time to be standing around waiting for the punch line of an interminable yarn. Kerrymen riddles are also very popular with children and young people and are the ideal medium for the exchange of quickfire humour and picking up the finer points of joke telling.

This is the biggest collection of Kerrymen riddles ever put together – over 500 in all. I can only hope that you have even half as much fun reading them as I had putting them together.

DES MACHALE

Have you heard about the Kerryman who got a pair of water skis for Christmas?
He's still going around looking for a lake with a slope.

What do you do to a one-armed Kerryman who is hanging from a tree?
Wave to him.

How do you play Kerry roulette?
You bang your head against the wall six times – once very hard.

In which month do Kerrymen drink the least?
February.

How do you recognise a Kerry string quartet?
Every five minutes they stop to clear the saliva from their instruments.

What do you call a Kerry policeman sitting up in a tree?
A Special Branch man.

Why did God create alcohol?
To stop Kerrymen from ruling the world.

Why do Kerrymen like underwater swimming?
Because deep down underneath they are quite intelligent.

How do you recognise a Kerryman on an oil rig?
He's the one throwing crusts of bread to the helicopters.

What is the happiest five-year period of a Kerryman's life?
Junior infants.

Why did the Kerryman cut a hole in his umbrella?
He wanted to know when it stopped raining.

What job did the Kerryman get in the navy?
Deckhand on a submarine.

What is the best thing that ever came out of Kerry?
The train to Dublin.

Why do Kerry policemen have numbers?
In case they get lost.

How do you recognise a Kerryman well versed in etiquette?
He doesn't blow his soup – he fans it with his cap.

Have you heard about the Kerryman who went to a mind reader?
He got his money back.

What happens when a Kerryman moves to Dublin?
He decreases the level of intelligence in both counties.

Have you heard about the Kerryman who pulled a fast one on Irish Rail?
He bought a return ticket to Dublin and never went back home again.

What is the capital of Kerry?
About £250.

Why do Kerry workers never go on strike?
Nobody would notice the difference.

What two Kerrymen didn't invent the aeroplane?
The Wrong brothers.

Why has Australia got all the kangaroos and Ireland got all the Kerrymen?
Australia had the first choice.

How do you recognise a Kerryman's matched luggage?
Two plastic bags from the same supermarket.

Why does a Kerryman put his budgie in a goldfish bowl?
When he puts it in a cage the water keeps coming out.

How do you recognise a Kerry nudist colony?
Men have blue ribbons in their hair while women have pink ribbons in their hair.

How do Kerrymen forge 10p pieces?
By filing the corners off 50p pieces.

What does a golfer get if he asks his Kerry caddie for a sand wedge?
Corned beef in brown bread.

How do we know that Santa Claus is from Kerry?
There are two doors and ten windows in the average house and he goes down the chimney.

What notice is prominently displayed on the door of Kerry restaurants?
CLOSED FOR LUNCH.

Why was the Kerryman walking down the road knocking down little old ladies and hitting children?
He was on his way to confession and didn't have enough sins to confess.

How do you recognise a Kerryman's video machine?
It records the programmes he doesn't want to see and shows them when he's out of the house.

Have you heard about the two Kerrymen who hijacked a submarine?
They demanded half a million pounds ransom and two parachutes.

At what Olympic events have Kerrymen won the most medals?
Heading the shot and catching the javelin.

Why did the Kerryman and his wife decide to have only three children?
They heard that every fourth child born is Chinese.

What do you call the shock absorbers in a Kerryman's car?
Passengers.

Have you heard about the Kerryman who owned a newspaper?
It cost him 70p.

Who is the odd man out in the following list?
Donald Duck, an intelligent Kerryman, the Archbishop of Canterbury and
King Kong.
The Archbishop of Canterbury – all the others are fictitious characters.

What do you see written on the front of a Kerry Mystery Tour bus?
DESTINATION CORK.

Why don't Kerrymen eat Smarties?
It's too much trouble peeling off the shells to get to the chocolate.

How do you sink a Kerry submarine?
Put it in water.

What happened to the Kerryman who bought washable wallpaper?
He'd only washed it twice when it was stolen from the clothesline.

Have you heard about the Kerryman who had two wooden legs?
Fire broke out in his house and he was burned to the ground.

What industrial action do Kerry circus employees take?
A go-slow on the Wall of Death.

Have you heard about the Kerryman who won the Tour de France?
He set off on a lap of honour and wasn't seen for a month.

What do the numbers 1914 and 1939 have in common?
Adjoining rooms in a Kerry hotel.

How would you get a Kerryman to climb onto the roof of a pub?
Tell him the drinks are on the house.

What is top of the bestseller list in Ireland this month?
Memoirs of a Kerry Kamikaze Pilot.

How do you recognise a Kerry cuckoo clock?
Every ten minutes the cuckoo pops its head out and asks the time.

How does a Kerryman cope with a gas leak?
He puts a bucket under it.

What did the Kerryman do when he saw a sign 'KEEP DEATH OFF THE ROADS'?
He drove his car on the footpath.

Have you heard about the Kerrywoman who bought *The Joy of Sex* for her husband for Christmas?
He coloured it in.

How do you recognise a Kerry typist?
Every time the little bell on her typewriter rings she takes a tea break.

Where is cleanliness next to Godliness?
In a Kerry dictionary.

What did the Kerry loan shark do when he lent out ten million pounds?
He immediately skipped town.

Have you heard about the Kerryman who fed and starved his pigs on alternate days?
He wanted to sell them for streaky bacon.

Why did the Kerryman have his sundial floodlit?
He wanted to be able to tell the time at night.

Have you heard about the Kerryman who bought a paper shop?
It blew away.

Is there a Kerry equivalent of mañana?
Yes, but it conveys nothing like the same sense of urgency.

What is a Kerry teacher's definition of an audio-visual aid?
Do you see this stick and do you hear what I'm saying?

What did the Kerryman do when he found his clothesline was too short?
He moved his house back ten feet.

How do you keep a Kerryman happy for an afternoon?
Write PTO on both sides of a piece of paper.

Have you heard about the two Kerry astronauts who went for a space walk?
They slammed the door of the spacecraft and left the key inside.

What happens to Kerry tadpoles?
They turn into butterflies.

Why did the Kerryman go into a second-hand shop?
To buy one for his watch.

How do you recognise a Kerryman's motor car?
Windscreen wipers on the inside.

Have you heard about the Kerry jellyfish?
It set.

How do you make a Kerry cocktail?
Take half a glass of whiskey and add it to another half a glass of whiskey.

Have you heard about the Kerry athlete who did a hundred metres in five seconds while wearing his wellies?
He fell over a cliff.

What is lesson one in a Kerry driving school?
How to open a locked car with a wire coat hanger.

Why do all Kerry football grounds have TV screens?
So the fans can see what is happening in their local bar.

Why did the Kerryman fail his driving test?
His car rolled forward on a hill start.

Why did the Kerryman return the dictionary he had just bought to the bookshop?
Because it didn't have an index.

Have you heard about the Kerry fire extinguisher factory?
It was burned to the ground.

What is the latest Kerry population control policy?
Shoot all the storks.

Have you heard about the Kerryman who invented the world's strongest glue?
He couldn't get the top off the bottle.

What is the Government warning on Kerry cigarette packets?
SMOKING SHORTENS YOUR CIGARETTES.

Have you heard about the Kerryman who was scared of heights?
He wouldn't go upstairs in a jumbo jet.

Why does a Kerryman take a box of matches to bed with him?
To see if he's turned out the light.

How do you recognise a Kerry topless restaurant?
It has no roof.

What is the definition of a smart Kerryman?
He's got an IQ.

Why did Kerry's top organist quit?
His monkey died.

Have you heard about the Kerryman who went surf riding?
His horse drowned.

How does a Kerryman avoid getting parking tickets?
He takes the windscreen wipers off his car.

What does the Kerry speaking clock say?
In precisely two seconds it will be nearly three o'clock.

What is the title of the bestselling sex manual in Kerry?
Brace Yourself Bridget.

Why was the Kerry Boat Race cancelled?
The course was waterlogged.

Have you heard about the Kerryman whose library was burned down?
Both books were destroyed and, worse still, one hadn't even been coloured in.

How do you get rid of a Kerry car?
Cover it with rust remover.

Why did the Kerryman go to London on his honeymoon, alone?
Because his wife had been to London before.

Have you heard about the Kerryman who was invited to a house-warming?
He spent the whole night helping to insulate the attic.

How do you recognise an hour-long Kerry sex video?
It's got one minute of sex followed by fifty-nine minutes of guilt.

What is white and goes upwards?
A Kerry snowflake.

Why did nineteen Kerrymen go to a film together?
Because they saw a notice UNDER 18 NOT ADMITTED.

What notice do you see in a Kerry public toilet?
Please do not eat the big polo mints in the urinals.

What is the definition of a fool?
Someone who drives into a Kerry garage and says 'Fill her up'.

How many Kerrymen does it take to milk a cow?
Twenty-four. One to hold each teat, and twenty to lift the cow up and down.

What award was given to the Kerryman who invented the silent alarm clock?
The Nobel Prize.

Why did the Kerryman rub liniment on his head?
He was told it would make him smart.

Have you heard about the Kerry farmer who went away for the weekend and forgot to unhitch one of his cows from the milking machine?
When he returned he found that the cow had been turned inside out.

How do you recognise a Kerry bullet-proof vest?
It has a money back guarantee if it doesn't work.

What is four miles long and has an IQ of forty?
A Kerry Saint Patrick's Day Parade.

Two Santas are standing outside a big store. Which one is the Kerryman?
The one with the bag of Easter eggs.

How do you recognise a Kerryman with an electric razor?
He's got the bathroom covered in foam.

Why did the Kerryman return his typewriter to the shop?
Because the keys weren't in alphabetical order.

What is a Kerry transistor?
A nun who wears mens' clothes.

Why did the Kerryman put his television set in the oven?
He wanted to make a TV dinner.

Have you heard about the Kerry rabbit who got caught by his leg in a trap?
He chewed off three of his legs but found he was still caught in the trap.

Why did the Kerry spacecraft crash?
It ran out of peat.

Why was the Kerryman pouring a gallon of Guinness down the toilet?
He was cutting out the middleman.

What are Kerry nurses famous for?
Waking patients up to take their sleeping tablets.

How does a Kerryman keep flies out of his kitchen?
He dumps a load of horse manure in his living-room.

How does a Kerryman lay underground telegraph cables?
First he digs thirty-foot holes for the telegraph poles.

Why did the Kerryman write to his broker?
He wanted a no claim bonus on his life insurance.

Have you heard about the latest Kerry invention for looking through solid walls?
It's called a window.

What happened to the Kerry Humpty Dumpty?
The wall fell on him.

Why did the Kerry goalkeeper never bother stopping the ball?
He thought that was what the net was for.

Why did the Kerry train driver lose his job?
For overtaking.

Have you heard about the expedition of Kerrymen who set out to climb Mount Everest?
They ran out of scaffolding thirty feet from the top.

Why did the Kerrywoman move from Tralee to Dingle?
She wanted to be nearer her son in New York.

What is green and drives to Dublin in reverse?
A Kerryman who knows the Highway Code backwards.

What does a Kerryman give an underweight parrot?
A packet of Pollyfilla.

Have you heard about the Kerry ghost?
He didn't believe in people.

What happened to the Kerry Leaning Tower?
It was straightened by a Kerry builder.

Where will you find toilet paper in a Kerry supermarket?
Under summer novelties.

What happened at the Kerry sheepdog trials?
All the dogs were found guilty.

What did the Kerry heart transplant patient do?
He sent a get well card to the donor.

Have you heard about the Kerryman who thought that VAT 69 was the Pope's telephone number?

What do you call a Kerryman driving a Mercedes?
A joy-rider.

Have you heard about the new parachute invented by a Kerryman?
It opens on impact.

What happened to the Kerry ice hockey team?
They drowned during spring training.

What do you call a Kerryman sitting in his back garden?
Paddy O'Furniture.

Have you heard about the Kerry hurricane?
It did £10 billion worth of improvements.

Have you heard about the Kerry clairvoyant?
He could look into the past.

What does a Kerryman take with him to a cock fight?
His duck.

How do you know if a Kerry cock fight is rigged?
The duck wins.

Have you heard about the Kerryman who lost all his luggage at Heuston Station?
The cork came out.

What happened to the Kerryman who tried to commit suicide by taking a hundred aspirins?
After he took two he began to feel better.

Why did the Kerryman lose his job as a barman?
He rinsed the ice-cubes in hot water and spent half an hour looking for them afterwards.

Have you heard about the Kerryman who ate twenty packets of corn-flakes?
He died of sunstroke.

Where would you find a Kerryman the day his boat comes in?
Waiting at the airport.

Why did the Kerryman take two hot water bottles to bed with him?
In case one of them sprang a leak.

What is the most outstanding achievement of the Kerry Minister for Defence?
Having de fence painted.

How did the four-foot Kerryman join the army?
He lied about his height.

What do you call a Kerryman in a detached house?
A squatter.

How do you recognise a Kerry gourmet?
He hangs the mince for a few days before cooking it.

Have you heard about the Kerry mosquito?
He caught malaria.

What organisation has the following uniform – a purple three cornered hat with a green feather, scarlet tunic, canary yellow trousers and pink sequined boots?
The Kerry Secret Service.

How do you recognise a Kerry waterproof watch?
It comes filled with water and you can't get it out no matter how hard you try.

What is the easiest way to get your name in print?
Just send £100 to the new *Kerry Directory of Confidence Trick Victims.*

Who is Kerry's most famous inventor?
Pat Pending.

How do you recognise a Kerryman at a drive-in movie?
If he doesn't like the show, he slashes the seats.

How do you disperse a crowd of Kerrymen in New York?
Shout 'immigration'.

How does a Kerry driver prepare for emergency stops?
He keeps the handbrake on all the time.

Have you heard about the Kerryman who won a trip to Japan in a raffle?
He's still out there trying to win a trip back.

What happens when you peel a Kerry onion?
It makes you laugh.

Have you heard about the Kerryman who died as a result of too much drink?
He was run over by a Guinness lorry.

Why did the Kerryman wear a wig with a big hole in the middle?
He figured that if he looked bald, people wouldn't realise he was wearing a wig.

Have you heard about the Kerryman who saw a 'Please mind the step' notice in a shop?
He had to wait over an hour until someone else came along to mind it for him.

Why do you never get ice in drinks in Kerry?
The fellow with the recipe emigrated.

What do you call a Kerryman's open convertible?
A skip.

Why do Kerry policemen always travel in threes?
One who can read, one who can write, and the third a special branch man
to keep an eye on two such dangerous intellectuals.

Have you heard about the Kerry ventriloquist?
His dummy quit to find a new partner.

What are the most popular courses at the Kerry Institute for Advanced
Studies?
Fractions and long division.

Have you heard about the famous Kerry dwarf?
At five feet he was the tallest dwarf in the world.

Why did the Kerryman visit the TV newsroom?
He wanted to know where they got all the ideas for the news.

Have you heard about the famous Kerry scientist Isaac MacNewton?
The apple tree fell on him and broke his neck.

How do you make a Kerryman laugh on Monday morning?
Tell him a joke on Friday evening.

How many Kerrymen does it take to change a light bulb?
Two. One says to the other, 'Could you switch the light on in here Mick?
It's so dark I can't see what I'm doing'.

Where would you find a Kerry woodpecker?
Exhausted on top of a brick.

Have you heard about the Kerryman who started a protection racket?
He threatened to beat people up if they paid him money.

What is the definition of an optimist?
A penniless Kerryman ordering oysters in a posh restaurant in the hope that he can pay the bill with the pearls.

What do you call a Kerryman on a bicycle?
A dope peddler.

Have you heard about the Kerry policeman who charged a motorist for having bald tyres?
The case was dismissed because it turned out that the fellow was driving a road roller.

How do you recognise a posh Kerryman?
He picks his nose with his little finger.

Have you heard about the Kerryman who bought a tube of the toothpaste with the stripes?
He wound up with alternate red and white teeth.

What did the Kerryman say when he saw the Eiffel Tower?
'They'll never get it off the ground'.

Have you heard about the Kerryman who locked his keys in his car?
It took him five hours to get his family out.

What happened to the Kerry Tug-of-War team?
They were disqualified for pushing.

How do you recognise a Kerry picket?
It goes on strike.

Have you heard about the Kerryman who spent an hour looking for a cap
in a big store?
He wanted one with a peak at the back.

Why was the Kerryman stranded for an hour in the supermarket?
The escalator broke down.

What has an IQ of 144?
A gross of Kerrymen.

What does a Kerry chiropodist have for breakfast?
Corn flakes.

How do you recognise a Kerry explorer?
Look in his kit for packets of dehydrated water.

What is the latest Kerry invention?
Ejector seats for helicopters.

Why did the Kerry comedian quit the stage?
Because people kept laughing at him.

How did the Kerry plastic surgeon meet his end?
He sat near the fire and melted.

Why did the Kerry boy swallow a £1 piece?
It was his lunch money.

Have you heard about the Kerryman who invented a new pill guaranteed to cure loss of memory?
He couldn't remember what it was for.

How do you recognise a Kerry card sharp?
He plays the one card trick.

How do you recognise a Kerry brothel?
It has bunk beds.

What were the last words of the Kerry gangster?
'Who put that fiddle in my violin case?'

How do you recognise a Kerry aircraft?
It's got outside toilets.

How do you get £100 from a Kerryman?

Ask him to lend you £200. Then say, 'Look, give me £100. Then you'll owe me £100, I'll owe you £100 and we'll be all square'.

Have you heard about the Kerryman who was told he would have to have a urine test?

He stayed up all night studying for it.

Have you heard about the Kerryman who used to eat nothing except paper clips?

His doctor had put him on a staple diet.

How do you recognise a Kerry mosquito?

It eats out of your hand.

Why didn't the Kerry miner have a light on his hat?

He was on the day shift.

What are old Kerry fire engines used for?
False alarms.

What is the definition of frustration?
A Kerry garage mechanic with greasy hands and no steering wheel to wipe them on.

What do you call a Kerryman who marries a gorilla?
A social climber.

What do you call a Kerryman who steals your drink?
Nick McGuinness.

Why did the Kerryman cross the road?
To get to the middle.
OK try again.
Why did the Kerryman cross the road?
Because it was the chicken's day off.

Have you heard about the Kerryman who stopped putting his clock forward every year?
It kept falling off the mantelpiece.

What did the Kerryman say when he was asked if he was a Catholic?
It's bad enough being an alcoholic.

What is compatibility for a Kerryman and his wife?
They both have headaches on the same night.

Have you heard about the Kerryman who refused to buy a Japanese radio?
He said he wouldn't be able to understand a word it said.

How do you brainwash a Kerryman?
Fill his wellies with water.

Why are there so many great Kerry pianists and so few great Kerry violinists?
Have you ever tried balancing a pint of Guinness on a violin?

Why did the Kerryman sue the bakery?
He claimed that they forged his signature on hot cross buns.

Have you heard about the Kerryman who stopped drinking?
He needed to belch.

Why did the Kerryman refuse to pay at the cinema?
Because he was only looking.

Have you heard about the Kerryman who went to England and made big money?
Unfortunately it was just a quarter of an inch too big.

What is the difference between a Kerry drunk and a Kerry alcoholic?
A Kerry drunk doesn't have to attend all those meetings.

What did the Kerryman say when he was told that the kangaroo was a native of Australia?
'To think that my sister married one of them things.'

Have you heard about the Kerryman who won the Nobel Prize for Agriculture?
He was simply a man out standing in his own field.

What do you call a Kerryman's car with twin exhausts?
A wheelbarrow.

What is the biggest educational problem in Kerry?
Kindergarten drop-out.

Have you heard about the latest Kerry invention?
A hairdryer which works under water.

Why didn't the Kerryman intervene when he saw an old lady struggling with four muggers?
He didn't know who had started it.

How do you recognise a Kerry Rubik cube?
All the faces are green and it takes only a few minutes to solve.

Have you heard about the Kerryman who got a job as coach with Manchester United?
He used to carry the team to away matches.

How many Kerrymen does it take to launch a ship?
A thousand and one – one to hold the bottle of champagne and a thousand to bang the ship against it.

What do you call a Kerryman's boomerang that won't come back?
A stick.

What did the Kerry Goldilocks say?
'Who's been sleeping in my porridge?'

Why did the Kerryman sew a label marked COTTON on his wool pull-over?
He thought it would fool the moths.

Have you heard about the Kerryman who had a degree in Computers and Art?
He got a job painting computers.

What is the latest Kerry invention?
A cure for wheatgerm.

How does a typical letter from a Kerryman to his Income Tax inspector read?
'Thanks for the offer, but I don't wish to join your club'.

What does a Kerryman say when he dials a wrong number to the person who answers?
'You fool, you've got the wrong number'.

What did the Kerryman do when his wife had twins?
He went out with a shotgun looking for the other man.

Have you heard about the Kerryman who crossed a dog with a tortoise?
It goes to the shop and brings back yesterday's newspaper.

Have you heard about the Kerry AAAA?
It's a new organisation for drunks who drive. Give them a ring and they will tow you away from the bar.

Have you heard about the Kerryman who was a director in the film business?
He had a job as a cinema usher.

What is the greatest achievement of the Kerry medical profession?
The world's first hernia transplant.

Have you heard about the new Kerry lottery?
First prize is a million pounds – one pound a year for a million years.

How do you recognise a Kerry formula one driver?
He makes a hundred pit stops – three for fuel, four for tyre changes and ninety-three to ask for directions.

What do you call a Kerryman under a wheelbarrow?
A mechanic.

What is the greatest achievement of the Kerry electronics industry?
They made the world's largest microchip.

What does the latest Kerry daredevil do?
He leaps over twenty motorcycles in a double decker bus.

Have you heard about the Kerry snake?
He fell in love with a coil of rope.

Have you heard about the Kerryman who caught a really big fish?
Its picture alone weighed twenty pounds.

What did the Kerryman do when his doctor told him to strip to the waist?
He took his trousers off.

How do you recognise Kerry identical twins?
They cannot tell each other apart.

What do you call a Kerryman's cordless razor?
A sheet of sand paper.

How do you recognise a Kerry mugger?
He gives his victims a business card in case they are ever in the same neighbourhood again.

Why did the Kerryman drive his new car over a cliff?
He wanted to test the air-brakes.

How do you recognise a Kerry ghost?
He jumps over walls.

Have you heard about the Kerry streaker?
He was taken to court but they couldn't pin a thing on him.

Why does a Kerry wake last three days?
To make sure the fellow is dead and not just dead drunk.

Have you heard about the Kerry hedgehog?
He fell in love with a hairbrush.

How do you recognise a Kerry central heating system?
It's got lagging jackets on the radiators.

Why do Kerry workers never get a tea-break?
It takes too long to retrain them afterwards.

Have you heard about the Kerry addict who quit the drug scene?
He tried sniffing coke but the bubbles kept going up his nose.

What do you do if a Kerryman throws a pin at you?
Run like mad; he's probably got a grenade between his teeth.

Why was the Kerryman reading a book called *How to Bring up Children?*
One of his kids had just fallen down a well.

Why was the Kerryman confused?
He couldn't understand how he had only three brothers while his sister had four.

How do you recognise a Kerry tortoise?
His shell has been recalled.

Have you heard about the Kerryman who set out to walk around the world?
He was drowned off Valentia Island.

What is the only part of a Kerryman's car that doesn't make a noise?
The horn.

What is reality to a Kerryman?
An illusion created by a lack of alcohol.

How do you recognise a Kerry pirate?
He's got a patch over each eye.

How does a Kerryman call his dog?
He puts two fingers in his mouth and shouts 'Rover'.

Where do Kerry babies come from?
You don't know? How does it feel to be dumber than a Kerryman?

How do you recognise a Kerry bathing suit?
Look for the label which says DRY CLEAN ONLY.

Have you heard about the Kerryman who completed a jigsaw in only six months?
He was very proud because it said '4 – 6 years' on the box.

Why is the average Kerryman like a lighthouse in the middle of a bog?
He's brilliant but useless.

What is the most accurate description of a Kerryman?
He's just a machine for turning potatoes into human nature.

How do you recognise a Kerry firing squad?
They stand in a circle so as not to miss.

How do you tell if the condemned man is from Kerry?
He doesn't duck.

What did the Kerryman say when the judge gave him 250 years in prison?
'If I hadn't a smart lawyer I'd have got life'.

Why did the Kerry grandmother go on the pill?
She didn't want to have any more grandchildren.

How do you sell a twenty pound hammer to a Kerryman?
Tell him it costs only ten pounds.

What is the definition of a true Kerryman?
Someone who would trample over the bodies of a dozen naked women to reach a pint of Guinness.

Why did the Kerry couple have a perfect marriage?
She didn't want to and he couldn't.

Why did the Kerrywoman give up breast-feeding?
After two feeds she ran out of breasts.

What is the most favoured Kerry sex position?
Woman underneath, man in the pub.

Have you heard about the Kerryman who had a brain transplant?
The brain rejected him.

Have you heard about the Kerry pilot who had an accident with his helicopter?
He thought it was a bit cold, so he turned the fan off.

What is the most popular sport in Kerry?
Turning Guinness into urine.

When the Kerryman lost his dog, why didn't he put an ad in the newspaper?
Because his dog couldn't read.

Why was the Kerryman jumping up and down on his way to work?
He had taken some medicine and forgotten to shake it beforehand.

Why was the Kerryman watering only half of his lawn?
Because the weather forecast said there was a 50% chance of rain.

Why were a hundred Kerry sailors drowned?
They were push-starting a submarine.

How do you recognise the bride at a Kerry wedding?
She's the one wearing the white wellies.

Why do Kerrymen's cars have such small steering wheels?
So they can drive with handcuffs on.

Where do Kerrymen go on holiday?
To a different bar.

Why did the Kerrywoman stop breast-feeding her baby?
It hurt too much when she boiled her nipples.

Why did the Kerryman refuse to accept a new telephone directory?
He hadn't finished reading the old one.

What did the Kerry couple do when their sex therapist told them that the best position was man on top and woman underneath?
They slept for two years in bunk beds.

Why did the Kerryman not drink his medicine after a hot bath?
By the time he had finished drinking the hot bath he hadn't room for any more.

Where do you look for Kerry wall-to-wall carpets?
All along the ceiling.

Why did the Kerry fisherman throw back a two-foot long fish?
His frying pan was only a foot wide.

Have you heard about the Kerry doctor who was treating a patient for jaundice for over three years?
He suddenly found out the fellow was Chinese. Worse still, he cured him.

For what are Kerry surgeons famous?
The difficult operation of appendix transplant.

Why do you never find salt cellars in Kerry?
It takes too long to fill them through the little hole in the top.

What does a Kerryman get if he multiplies 314159 by 271828?
The wrong answer.

Why did the Kerryman buy 37 tickets when going to the cinema?
Some fellow inside the door kept tearing them up.

What did the Kerryman do when he saw a notice outside the police station MAN WANTED FOR ARMED ROBBERY?
He went in and applied for the job.

How do you recognise a bath made in Kerry?
It's got taps at both ends to keep the water level.

Why did the Kerry one-man bus crash?
The driver was upstairs collecting fares at the time.

What happens to a girl who goes out with a Kerryman for an evening?
Nothing.

Why was the Kerryman disqualified from the walking race?
Because he won it two years running.

Why did the Kerry level crossing have one gate open and one gate closed?
They were half expecting a train.

How do you tell a Kerryman joke to a Kerryman?
Very slowly.

Have you heard about the Kerryman who tried to hijack an aircraft?
He planted a bomb in the plane and gave the pilot five minutes to leave the cabin.

What are the secret plans for the Kerry rocket to the sun?
They're sending it at night.

How are Kerry flights announced at the airport?
The next flight for Kerry will leave when the big hand is at the two and the little hand is at the six.

Why did the Kerryman open the door of his car while taking his driving test?
He wanted to let the clutch out.

Why do Kerrymen not use local anaesthetics?
They think the imported ones are better.

Why did the Kerrymen visit the famous Harley Street plastic surgeon?
To have his plastic bucket mended.

What was the message received by the Kerry deep-sea diver?
'Come up immediately, we're sinking'.

Why did the Kerryman learn to cut his fingernails with his left hand?
In case he ever lost his right.

Why did the Kerryman's rope have only one end?
Because he cut the other end off.

What do you find on the bottom of Kerry beer bottles?
OPEN OTHER END.

How do you recognise a Kerry shoplifter?
He steals free samples.

How does a Kerryman tell his twin sons Mick and John apart?
He puts his finger in Mick's mouth and if he bites him he knows it's John.

Have you heard about the Kerryman who got a job as quality control officer in a banana factory?
They had to let him go because he kept throwing away all the ones that were crooked.

Why did the Kerryman who was being executed refuse a last cigarette?
Because he was trying to give them up.

Why was the Kerryman committing suicide with a rope round his waist?
When it was around his neck it was choking him.

Why did the Kerryman want a train ticket for Jeopardy?
Because he heard that there were 500 jobs in jeopardy.

How do you recognise a Kerry football referee?
He plays extra time before the match in case there is fog.

Why did the Kerryman buy a black and white dog?
He figured that the licence would be cheaper than for a coloured one.

Why did the Kerry spider stop spinning webs?
Because he lost his pattern book.

How do you recognise a Kerry chocolate?
It melts in your hand, not in your mouth.

Why was the Kerryman pushing his bike to work?
He was so late he didn't even have time to get on it.

How do you recognise a Kerry sundial?
It loses ten minutes a day.

Why did the Kerryman think that TV programmes had improved greatly?
His wife had rearranged the furniture and he was watching the fish tank.

What did the Kerryman say when the doctor told him he had German measles?
'But I've never even been to Germany'.

What is the bestselling game in Kerry at Christmas?
The one-piece jigsaw.

When do Kerrymen find the one-piece jigsaw difficult?
When they lose the top of the jigsaw box with the picture on it.

How do you recognise a superstitious Kerryman?
He won't work on any week with a Friday in it.

Why did the Kerryman give up water polo?
His horse drowned.

What was the Kerryman studying at medical school?
Nothing – they were studying him.

Who is ten feet tall and lives in Kerry?
Paddy Long Legs.

How do you recognise a Kerry carpet in mint condition?
It's got a hole in the middle.

How did the Kerryman bite himself on the forehead?
He stood on a chair.

How do you recognise a Kerry obscene telephone call?
Heavy belching.

What is the definition of an intellectual Kerryman?
One who goes to an art gallery even when it's not raining.

How do you recognise a Kerry raffle?
Tickets are £1 each or a book of 10 for £11.

Why does a Kerryman carry a bomb in his suitcase when flying to London?
Because he figures that the chances of two people carrying bombs in their suitcases on the same flight is virtually nil.

Why did the Kerryman stipulate that there should be no flowers at his funeral?
He was allergic to them.

How does a Kerry doctor console a Kerry widow?
Thank God he didn't die of anything serious.

Have you heard about the Kerry crematorium?
It caught fire and all the bodies were burned to death.

Why are Kerry snow-ploughs so useless?
The drivers refuse to operate them when the weather is really bad.

How do you recognise a top Kerry business executive?
He's the one wearing pin-striped wellies.

Have you heard about the Kerryman's dog who was sitting by the fire chewing a bone?
When he got up he realised he had only three legs.

What did the Kerryman choose as his special subject on MASTERMIND?
Polish Popes of the twentieth century.

What is a Kerryman's favourite drink?
The next one.

Why did the Kerryman eat Tampax?
Because he wanted to be able to swim, ski and even parachute at any time of the month.

What is the bestselling Kerry cookbook?
365 Ways to Cook a Potato.

What would a Kerryman be if he wasn't a Kerryman?
Ashamed of himself.

What is the withdrawal policy of a Kerry bank?
You can draw your money out at any instant provided you give two weeks notice.

Why was there a delay in introducing decimal currency into Kerry?
They were waiting for all the old people to die.

What do you call a Kerryman who rides his bicycle on the pavement?
A psychopath.

What happens to a Kerryman who doesn't pay his garbage bill?
They stop delivering.

What do you call a Kerryman who knows how to control a wife?
A bachelor.

How do you recognise a Kerry engagement ring?
It's got three rubies, a sapphire, and two diamonds – all missing.

Why are Kerrymen such poor card players?
Every time they pick up a spade, they spit on their hands.

When were the good old days in Kerry?
When you could go into a restaurant with £1, get a meal, a drink and a good overcoat.

Have you heard about the Kerryman who invented an electric car and drove from Tralee to Dublin?
The electricity cost him only £5 but the extension cord cost him £100,000.

What did the Kerryman say the first time he saw a lobster pot?
'How would you get a lobster to sit on one of those things?'

Why was the Kerryman's house hit by a Jumbo jet?
He left the landing light on.

Why couldn't the Kerryman read the daily newspaper?
Because he had gone to night school.

Have you heard about the Kerry skunk?
He fell in love with a gas leak.

Why was the Kerry forger arrested?
He was caught with ten million nine pound notes.

What is every Kerry burglar's ambition?
To learn how to pick the locks of pay toilets.

How do you recognise a Kerryman's watch?
It can do an hour in forty-five minutes.

Why was the Kerryman painting his house at a furious rate?
He wanted to finish before the paint ran out.

How do you recognise a £20 note forged by a Kerryman?
Look for the words ILLEGAL TENDER.

What do you call a brick on a Kerryman's head?
An extension.

Why did the Kerry prisoner who tunnelled his way out of jail give himself up to the police?
He told them he was only practising for the mass breakout at the end of the month.

Why was boxing never popular in Kerry?
Nobody could count.

Why was the Kerryman laughing hysterically as he was to be hanged?
Because they were hanging the wrong man.

What is the favourite sport in Kerry small towns?
Watching the local alcoholic having delirium tremens.

Have you heard about the Kerrywoman who tried to iron her curtains?
She fell out the window.

What is the most popular dish in Kerry restaurants?
Soup in the basket.

What did the Kerryman think when he saw a roll of sellotape?
He thought it was a glue sniffer's packed lunch.

Have you heard about the Kerryman who bet that he could lean further
out the window than his brother?
He won.

What do you call a 300 pound Kerryman with a sawn off shotgun?
Sir!

What is the bestselling girlie magazine in Kerry?
Ploughboy.

How do you make a Kerrywoman pregnant?
You don't know? And you think Kerrymen are dumb!

What do you call a Kerryman with 6 honours in his Leaving Cert?
A liar.

Why did the Kerry psychiatrist put his wife under the bed?
He thought she was just a little potty.

What did the Kerryman say when the judge offered him thirty days or a hundred pounds?
'I'll take the hundred pounds'.

What is the definition of a true Kerryman?
Someone who goes to a topless bar just to get drunk.

Why do Kerry businessmen not take coffee after lunch?
It keeps them awake all afternoon.

How do you recognise a Kerry polo mint?
The hole is on the outside.

How does a Kerry photographer manage if he hasn't got a darkroom?
He just wears a blindfold.

How much do haircuts cost in Kerry?
£8 – £2 a corner.

What do you call a Kerryman hanging from the ceiling?
Seán D'Olier.

How do you recognise a Kerry mousetrap?
It comes complete with its own mice.

How do you recognise a formal Kerry dinner?
When all the men come to the table with their flies zipped up.

What do you call a Kerryman who carries only a sawn off shotgun and a switchblade?
A pacifist.

Have you heard about the Kerry karate expert?
He killed himself saluting.

How do you know if you are being mugged by a Kerryman?
You have to show him what to do.

How does a Kerryman call a cab?
He puts his fingers in his mouth and shouts 'Taxi!'

What did the Kerryman say when he went to the ballet for the first time?
'Why don't they get taller girls?'

What does a Kerry bank clerk say when you hand him money?
'For me?'

What do you find at the top of a Kerry ladder?
A STOP sign.

How do you recognise a Kerryman's roll of toilet paper?
Look for the instructions printed on every sheet.

Why was the Kerryman standing in front of the mirror with his eyes closed?
He wanted to see what he looked like when he was asleep.

What did the Kerryman say when he saw a moose head on a wall?
'He must have been going at a fair old pace when he hit that wall'.

Why did the Kerryman spend two hours in a revolving door?
He was trying to slam it.

Have you heard about the Kerryman who kept reading that cigarette smoking was bad for him?
He gave up reading.

Why are there so few champion Kerry skiers?
They cannot get their pants on over their skis.

How many Kerrymen does it take to hang a picture?
Thirty-one to hold the ladder, one to hold the screw, and twenty-eight to turn the wall around.

What does a Kerryman say while reading a newspaper?
'Isn't it amazing how people always seem to die in alphabetical order.'

Have you heard about the Kerry girl who came second in a beauty contest?
She was the only entrant.

What is the difference between a Kerry wake and a Kerry wedding?
A Kerry wake has one less drunk.

What does a Kerryman say when he sees a man playing the trombone?
'There must be some trick to it – he can't really be swallowing it.'

Why did the Kerryman buy a house next to the pawnshop?
So he could keep an eye on his property.

Why did the Kerry farmer hitch his prize bull to a plough?
He wanted to show him that there was more to life than romance.

What do you call a Kerryman who keeps bouncing his head off the wall?
Rick O'Shea.

Have you heard about the Kerry turkey?
He was looking forward to Christmas.

How did the gang of robbers escape from a Kerry superstore?
The police had surrounded all of the exits so they must have escaped through an entrance.

Why did the Kerryman take his pregnant wife to the supermarket?
He heard they made free deliveries.

How do you recognise a Kerry car pool?
They all meet at work.

Why did the Kerryman shoot his packet of cornflakes?
He was a cereal killer.

How do you recognise a Kerry intellectual?
He can read without moving his lips.

Why did the bald Kerryman refuse to have a transplant?
He thought he'd look daft with a kidney on his head.

Have you heard about the Kerryman who tried to commit suicide with an elastic rope?
He died of concussion.

What happened to the Kerryman who tried to blow up a bus?
He burned his lips on the exhaust pipe.

How does a Kerryman do a 'Spot the Ball' entry?
He prods around his newspaper with a pin until he hears 'psst'.

Why do Kerry elephants drink?
It helps them to forget.

How do you keep Kerrymen out of your house?
Hide the key under a bar of soap.

Have you heard about the Kerryman who joined the Mafia?
They made him an offer he couldn't understand.

What do you call a Kerryman in a semi-detached house?
A burglar!

How do you recognise a really classy Kerryman?
All the words on his tattoo are spelled correctly.

What does a Kerryman call his pet zebra?
Spot.

What did the Kerryman do when his pet canary lost its sight in an accident?
He took it to the Bird's Eye factory.

Why did the Kerryman quit his job as a taxi-driver?
He couldn't stand people talking behind his back.

How do you confuse a Kerryman?
Put him in a barrel and tell him to stand in a corner.

What did the Kerryman do when he heard that 90% of car accidents happen within five miles of home?
He moved house.

How do you recognise a posh Kerry household?
They have grapes even when nobody is sick.

Why did the Kerryman quit his job as a fireman?
It used to take him nearly two hours to slide back up the pole.

Why do Kerrymen carry umbrellas when it's not raining?
Because umbrellas can't walk!

What do you get if you cross a Kerryman with an elephant?
A Kerryman who will never forget you, a dirty look from the elephant, and the Nobel prize for biology.

How many Kerrymen does it take to carry out a kidnapping?
Ten – one to capture the kid and nine to write the ransom note.

Why do Kerrymen wear bowler hats?
To protect their heads from woodpeckers.

Have you heard about the Kerryman who does wonderful work for hospitals?
He makes people sick.

Have you heard about the Kerryman who died in China?
They buried him in a paddy-field!

Have you heard about the Kerryman who lost £10 on the Grand National?
Worse still, he lost £20 on the television re-run.

Have you heard about the Kerry seaside village that was reputed to be the dullest place in the world?
One day the tide went out and never came back in again.

Why did the Kerryman set fire to his jacket?
He wanted a blazer.

What did the Kerry fatted calf say when he saw the Prodigal Son coming over the hill?
'O goody, here comes the Prodigal Son'.

How do you sink a Kerry submarine?
Knock on the door.

What does a Kerryman say while making an obscene telephone call?
'Stop telling me the time while I'm talking to you'.

What happened when Kerry grave-diggers went on strike?
There was a wave of panic dying.

Why do Kerrymen never take their wives out?
Their mothers warn them not to go out with married women.

What does a Kerryman take for a headache?
Nothing – because nothing acts faster than Anadin.

How do you recognise the instruction manual for a Kerry car?
Easy – it's a bus timetable.

What do you call a Kerryman with his ears stuffed with cotton wool?
Anything you like – he can't hear you.

How does the system of yellow lines on Kerry streets operate?
One yellow line means no parking at all. Two yellow lines mean no parking at all at all.

What do you call a Kerryman in a suit?
The defendant.

Have you heard about the Kerry chess champion?
He played blindfold against twelve Soviet Grandmasters simultaneously and was annihilated in all twelve matches.

Why did the Kerryman spend three hours in a carwash?
He thought it was raining too hard to drive.

Why does a Kerryman's car have heated rear windows?
To keep his hands warm while he is pushing it.

How do you recognise a Kerryman's pencil?
It's got an eraser at both ends.

How do you recognise a Kerryman's word processor?
The screen is covered in Tippex.

Why did the Kerryman drive his car into a lake?
He was trying to dip his headlights.

What does a Kerry blacksmith say to his assistant?
'I'll put the red-hot iron on the anvil and when I nod my head, you hit it.'

Have you heard about the Kerry acid bath murderer?
He lost an arm taking the stopper out of the plughole.

Why did the Kerryman lose his job as a lift operator?
He couldn't remember his route.

Why was the Kerryman jumping up and down on a hedgehog?
He wanted a really big conker.

What is the infallible Kerry cure for seasickness?
Sit under a tree.

How did the Kerryman injure himself at a Halloween party?
He was bobbing for chips.

What happened to the Kerry tap-dancer?
He got washed down the sink.

Why did the Kerry explorer pay £20 for a sheet of sandpaper?
He thought it was a map of the Sahara Desert.

Have you heard about the Kerry burglar who went to America?
He was caught stealing the lead off the roof of Fort Knox.

Have you heard about the Kerry kidnapper who was picked up by the police?
He enclosed a stamped addressed envelope with the ransom note.

What does a Kerry photographer do with his burned out light bulbs?
He uses them in his darkroom.

How do you double the value of a Kerryman's car?
Fill the tank with petrol.

What is the Kerry cure for water on the brain?
A tap on the head.

What is the Kerry cure for water on the knee?
Drainpipe trousers.

When do little Kerry boys play truant from school?
Saturday.

What did the Kerryman do when he got a pair of cuff-links for Christmas?
He went and had his wrists pierced.

How do you recognise a Kerryman's crystal tableware?
Two empty jars of the same brand of peanut butter.

Have you heard about the Kerryman who became a streaker?
He ran fully clothed through a nudist colony.

How long does it take a Kerryman to write a note to the milkman?
About an hour – even longer if he forgets to write on the paper before he puts it into the bottle.

Have you heard about the Kerryman who tunnelled his way to freedom from prison in two months?
He was serving only one month.

What is the best time to sell land to a Kerryman?
When the tide is out.

Have you heard about the Kerryman who committed suicide by drinking a can of varnish?
He had a terrible end but a beautiful finish.

How many Kerrymen does it take to make popcorn?
Ten – one to hold the pan and nine to shake the cooker up and down.

What happened to the Kerry cannibal who went on a self-catering holiday?
He came back with two wooden legs.